D0194152

# Lessons for Tangueros

by

## Lew Watts

authorHOUSE®

*AuthorHouse™*
*1663 Liberty Drive*
*Bloomington, IN 47403*
*www.authorhouse.com*
*Phone: 1-800-839-8640*

*First published by AuthorHouse     2/14/2011*

*ISBN: 978-1-4567-1004-0 (e)*
*ISBN: 978-1-4567-1005-7 (sc)*

*Library of Congress Control Number: 2010917110*

*Printed in the United States of America*

*This book is printed on acid-free paper.*

*Certain stock imagery © Thinkstock.*

she declines his glance
with a slow turn of the head
moment of death

# Contents

## Before

## Lessons

## Steps

## Reflections

## Acknowledgements

# Before

# Black Tie Lament

When we used to dance we stayed apart,
thrashing and shaking our heads as though denying

we'd get to an age where the only time we'd touch
was when I'd cup your elbow through a door,

or dab dust from your eye with a handkerchief,
or push the small of your back away from a fracas.

Your father taught you to ballroom dance - a shame
I never knew him, learned to quick-step. Instead,

in these black-tie benefit years of life,
I look away when I hear you tap your feet

under the table unable to catch my eye;
then dancing with your purse or another man

while in the washroom I wash the room for hours,
willing down at my hairline, picking teeth.

But there is always one last dance, some crap like Andy
Williams' *Wise Men Say Only Fools Rush In* -

and I'm back tapping her to dance, catching her gum,
lifting her arms around my neck, swooning slower

than a 45 of *I'm Not in Love* played 33.
And later when she's stepping on my feet,

walking like two clowns across her room,
we rhumba out of clothes and into sheets -

and there you are, mincing in your stilettos
in a "slow-slow-quick/quick-slow" way,

wrapping yourself in frenzied figures of eight
which unravel like the strands of a skein of wool

before we reach the car. When I turn the key,
for the first time that night I feel a hero.

# Sapphic Dreams of Dancing with You

In my dreams you're looking behind a curtain,
Searching for the husband you walked away from,
Lured by his *Hecaterus* hands that slowly
Move in the shadows,

Waiting all those years to embrace and make up,
Framed within the space which you left that evening,
Sliding back to fox-trot and walz and rhumba
Into your past life.

Sometimes I can stop you before the music
Draws you through its veil of allure by calling
Out your name. It's always the same - this destined
Distance between us.

So it seemed until the silence was broken
One night when you opened your wings and sirens
Signalled *Terpsichore's* arrival. And I
Danced for the first time.

# Bandoneón

The first time that I heard it was in Grace
Jones' *I've seen your face before*, borrowed
from Piazzolla's masterpiece, amazed
the notes could drown a honeymoon in sorrow.
                    -/-
Thank God they dropped the name *Reinische Tonlage*,
to honor Heinrich Band. According to some,
German sailors brought them rather than larger
koncertinas - *not* accordions

with their piano keys; only buttons,
71 to be precise, with separate
notes on push and pull, the mellow butter
tones from pairs of reeds an octave apart.
                    -/-
In early days it served to keep a beat
behind the bass before it rose and claimed
tango's soul when Troilo let the beast
sing his troubled song and share his pain.

Draped across the knees it seems alive,
writhing like a snake to escape the lap
of its stenographer. His taps transcribe
its lithe strength, his hands trapped in straps.
                    -/-
When you would turn your hip away Yvonne,
I'd use the night to play our elegy,
watching the embers die to bandoneón
greats, save one - the greatest tragedy.

Born in 1900, she rose to fame
against all odds. Her 15 tango scores
are all that's left except her face - her name?
Francisca Pacquito. She died at 24.

# An Orchestra of Voices for Astor Piazzolla

*Argentine Tango is traditionally danced to recordings made in the "classic period" of the 1930s and 40s. In some milongas (formal dances), more modern or contemporary music is deemed inappropriate. Piazzolla, the greatest exponent of nuevo tango, wrote Adiós Nonino in the days following the death of his father..*

Born of Argentinian blood,
raised between the streets of the Bronx,
you found your voice in the buttons
of your beloved bandoneon.

When you returned to Buenos Aires,
already famous, flush with success,
you were almost placed under arrest
for shaming tango, a tarnished guest.

So let us ask

Eduardo Donato, Julio de Caro,
Osvaldo Pugliese, Osvaldo Fresedo,
Quinteto Piricho, Anibal Troilo
(your bandoneon God, *Pichicu*),
Roberto Firpo, Elvino Vardaro,
Alfredo Lorenz, Pedro Mafia
Alfredo Gobi, Adolfo Carabelli,
Ciriaco Ortiz, Juan d'Arienzo,
Carlos de Sarli, Carlos Marcucci,
and Carlos Gardel, who sings ...

Our country's greatest shame was yet
to come. Now past, we lie here longing
for the world to mourn each tortured death
and write an *Adiós Nonino*.

# Tango!

*A tanguera is a female tango dancer*

Looking back, the book was just a book
of facts. The only time emotion showed
was with the exclamation mark that bullied

*Tango* into tabloid print, as though
it was "all you wanted to know, roll-
up-roll-up, read and gloat at the bowed

heads - *tanguera* lost her throat and soul
to dark stranger in a close embrace".
Instead, we learn in Chapter 1 that tango

arose in the arrabals of Buenos Aires
as a dance for men deranged for lack of women;
later as a way to learn the grace

of respect and etiquette. I didn't know in
tango no one speaks within the dance -
as though they still recall when it was a sin -

and every invitation starts with a glance
awaiting the nod. The man is not the 'lead'
but indicates with a shift of weight ... it's jazz -

improvized, each sequence never repeats,
never repeats the last entangled image,
moving beyond the rhythm of a heart beat,
like the endless wonder of turning a page.

# I want to change my life

So long coming this moment swollen like a river eternity before the click before the click kicks in, blue name beckoning just a click away from the website image he looming against some wall in an alleyway called Heaven she leaning back skirt splintered to her hip leg wrapped around his violation. Call the number. "Yes? - this is he" - *I want* ... "Why not do one as a trial, alright with you?" - always not that I would want *to change* my thimble prick your outer shell and watch you blunt me always harder than the coins paid with a whimper. "Have you ever?" - no never never sensed the scent of a vertical woman never felt a body move towards my hands or turned to see a face dropped in trust instead of faces turned. "You need leather soles so you can turn" - and I thought how prescient my future teacher for the night devils turn as fresh as babies screaming their way to wet attention piercing the hardest soul. "$70 for a single lesson" - and so it is almost done just a touch would be enough to be touched a bonus. (But what if my mouth dries open or the lump in my throat moves to my groin or I sweat that acrid sweat you hated or my feet rise into my arms?) "One final question" - ask the one the one about *my life* click on my own blue line chink this armor my amor sound the dull alarm of "why?" you aways asked me this even when we'd both been taken by others. "Do you?" - almost always almost ever since the call that said you'd died I never had to say a word. "Want?" - often but desire is all I really crave. "To dance?" - ah there's a thing come closer now and feel my temples beat. "Tango?" - heroic nights falling into each other falling in valor falling for each other.

And I am back within the deep reaches far upstream where one day the water was clear before she rained and rained. And I am trying to stand but the sand is bleeding through my feet shifting me into her current. Life is always like this neither drifting nor swimming just the slow draw downstream passed from hand to mouth into the mouth of flooded protests. And when the eddies slow I dream I am allowed to crawl out onto a pristine bar lying there in the timelessness of it all staring at the inevitable sky until the breath dies naturally with a whisper. But it's all too exposed too much to share before I'm back in water where I am someone else or not. The question stays on the line until the answer comes out slowly at first like a tide up the throat over the tongue and then so fast it can't be caught until it's in almost in the open. I want to say it I want to say but I am long gone back in the stream pulling with the current but I say *I want to surprise my wife.* "Yeah right, that's nice" - strange the way our secrets rhyme just like the title of this poem so long coming.

# Lessons

# The First Lesson

If I remember rightly you were late
which didn't seem to bother you at all.
Her fated name was Mary; she was tall,
with 4" heels. You should have checked my height

or given me a box to stand upon,
or told her that her low-cut dress would draw
my nose towards her mottled cleft. Or
you could have let me sweat and fret alone.

The tin of mints you left out on the bench
would normally have been a hint. It was
too subtle for my rancid breath because
I smothered her with garlic's acrid stench.

And how was I to know that in embrace
you never grip the kidneys, nor should you
chip her painted toes or crush her shoes? -
those *Comme il Fauts*! Her limp was my disgrace.

My shirt was wet. My feet were glued to the wall -
those rubber soles, their syncopated squeak
beyond all forms of life or tango beat.
In one long hour I only learned to walk.

# The Second Lesson

You told me that it made you strong
in the months after you had died.
And me thinking all along,
that they were love-bites, on the side
of the neck, the left, I always chase
when not in close embrace.

I now know why I came again.
It was the way they danced, her prize
at the end of a long lesson of pain,
the locked trance beneath stilled eyes,
the subtle shift of shoulder, and at once
the sleek slide of response.

But there I was in the same room,
the square block wooden tiles
polished by a thousand tunes,
when you walked in flushed and tired,
your hair tied up over silk and muslin
and that Arabic scent of the hunted.

And watching you slip your feet into shoes,
strapping your ankles with a soft click,
then rising up with a sigh, smoothing
your palms over your lap and hips.
We walked a hundred miles, me leading
you forever receding.

So that when he showed me those first crucial
three steps to the left of you with a twist
that brought you to the cross, *cruzada*,
the tango sign of chastity,
in that moment I owned your axis,
to pivot you to exit.

13

Then at Bistro du Coin, on Connecticut,
you had a coffee to my martini
and told me over nicotine
of the drug-crazed builder who used his key
and cut you deeply with a knife
to the edge of night.

They lost you in the ambulance
but, wrapped inside your flowing shawl,
you turned away from Ridwan's call
and, in the following days, your veins lanced,
you ground your teeth to the shape of a saw,
serrated like your scars.

So it was only a matter of time before
I would see you lying on the floor,
and would take your half-severed hand
and lift you up as you told me of tango,
of the life of the dance and the blood rush,
amid the fear of touch.

# The Fourth Lesson - Shoes

My tango shoes arrived,
a pair of Werner-Kerns!
I need to come to terms
with soles of polished suede.

We step out on the floor,
the music starts on cue,
you said you thought it cute
the way I slid out through the door.

# The Fifth Lesson - Molinette

*Also known as Giro, a Molinette (fan) is a tango figure in which
the lady dances around the man, stepping side-back-side-forward.*

"Imagine there's a tray across your arms.
Now when you're ready, place your foot behind
the other heel - turn your frame, collect."
And as you turn she traces out a fan,
her face and eyes for you alone as she winds
a silken thread within a *molinette*.
That's how it was when I watched the way you moved,
coiling your foot to oil the spin, the neat
whip of hips.
Then she who has nightly dined
on tango meat is forced to fake a smooth
glide within my metronomic beat,
sipping from a shaking crock of wine
this waiter holds - so dumb these clockwork feet.
The key rotates, grinding the bones of my spine.

# The Group Lesson

*In group tango lessons, roles are reversed in that ladies
rotate from man to man with each new set.*

It's only practice, but practice for what
lies beyond a lowered gaze and face
turned away from me. The key is not
thinking I'm just another man I hate.

Lies, beyond a lowered gaze and face,
are your eyes closed in each embrace as though
thinking I'm just another man. I hate
watching you in another's arms, I know.

Are your eyes closed in each embrace, as though
turned away from me? The key is not
watching you in another's arms. I know
it's only practice - but practice for what?

# The First Practica

*Unlike a formal tango milonga, a practica is an opportunity
to practice - dancers can stop and repeat steps amid an
atmosphere where experts and beginners dance and learn ...*

In the cluttered gloom of the public library,
pushed to the side of back-lists of the dead,
they gather in a side-room every Saturday
to strut and preen or practice. I had dreaded
this glut of cold anxious lives disguised
within the cauldron of a *practica*
where each new prey is sliced and analyzed
while in the wash-room jilted ladies bicker.

I have to thank you Jaime for those words
you whispered as I watched her storm away,
but at the time they seemed to me absurd
and only later did I learn to say
this saving phrase, my macho tango mantra
each time I missed a step or went for glory
and failed to keep my frame. Your simple answer -
*tangueros never ever say they're sorry.*

# A Triolet for Tango Wounds

*A tanguero is a male tango dancer*

It's strange that you would recommend to me
a guest-house where tangueros wounds are healed
for, after being shunned like fetid meat,
it's strange that you would recommend. To me,
to visit Buenos Aires for one meagre
dance within a widow's arms ... really,
it's strange that you would. Recommend to me
a guest house where tangueros wounds are healed.

# The Tenth Lesson

It might have been the fact that
I came into the room and found you
dancing together, your hair matted
with sweat, your shirts soaked through.

Or that he let you rest your feet
while leading me by the hand in terror.
And all I could think of was the heat
in my cheeks, and his muscles in the mirror.

I led, he moved, we tripped and fell
close to your lap. My eyes welled
and dripped staccato drops as I prayed,
my hands on the floor, the urge to bray

and throw my head back and shout to all

who laughed and laugh
at this sacrificial calf
at tango's alter
with the weight of assault
heavy on the bowels of shame
until my dignity came
back
in black.

Standing in humiliated splendor
I told him that the lesson was over.

# The First Milonga

*A milonga is a formal tango dance*

To fortify myself I ate roast beef
on the many nights I stayed alone at home,
market-fresh, the loin hung like a wreath
until the final rib and then there was none.

You promised me it was a friendly place,
used to rank beginners - you were certain
alcohol was served with nuts on plates.
I climbed the stairs and drew apart the curtain.

I took an empty chair by the piano,
whiling the time with wine, re-tying laces,
then moving out of sight within the shadows
behind a row of silent painted ladies.

You entered in a breeze - so many kisses
blown across the room - your hair flowered,
your feet already saddled, you were whisked
beyond my saddened eyes onto the floor.

And then I saw the terrifying theme -
for every man there were a dozen women
like lines of flowers longing for a bee
to fertilize their hands and stroke their stamens.

The panic turned to sweat, a quick descent
to total desolation. Then alone,
his tail between his legs, this little pig went
pissing and peeing all the way home.

# Obsession

*In Argentine tango, a tanda is a set of pieces of music -*
*usually 3 to 5 - after which there is a short break.*

I don't suppose you'll ever understand.
Why would you when all tango music grates
and grinds your bones to dust, and clouds are gray -
they're never white - and *why?* is a verbal hand-
slap when I tap my feet through a complete tanda?
For you, the evening warmth is a silence game,
with a homely partner by your side, stayed
by strings to his wings, lashed and grounded to land.
But I even hear its rhythm in the dish-
washer and in the ring-tone on my phone.
And when I walk in Wholefoods there's pride
of step and an urge to spin the cashier. This
is where I really go, dancing alone,
much worse than having a guilty smoke outside.

# Rondeau for Tangueros

Within the dance are lows and highs
from women ready to chastise
your swollen feet, and heap all shame
on you for any ankles maimed
within the dance.

But these same ladies can surprise
you with their thighs, with silent sighs
and flashing lashes, eyes aflame
within the dance.

But you must learn to exorcise
all doubt and demons; otherwise,
they'll wince and mince and baste the blame
on any guy who breaks his frame -
retaliating is unwise
within the dance.

# Embrace

They didn't even argue any more,
except at formal dinners, for as much
as he would try he couldn't dance at all -
they'd lost their youth and now their sense of touch.
He kept his lessons secret, even when
they fell apart - the long walks home from bad
nights were the worst. Within his garden den
he hid his shoes inside a fishing bag.
But then, one night, on a terrace in Key Largo
he took her hand and watched her look of dread
fall away as he led her in a tango,
savoring the skin beneath her dress.
It was the second time he'd held his wife;
the first was when they wed - a 60s jive.

# Steps

# Salida

*In Argentine tango, Salida can be either an exit from a figure,*
*or the entrance to the dance itself. A Parada is a stop,*
*sometimes held by the side of the leader's foot*

Like a youth who brings a girlfriend to the brink
of a windswept cliff, her lips wet with desire,
you concentrate and wait to be inspired,
but nothing comes except a chill that brings

an ache. The dance had started well, I thought,
the standard opening with the classic eight
steps and, as you turned, added weight,
setting a stopped *parada* with my foot.

By the time you caught my eye the melody
had gone beyond its melancholic pause
when, after being snared, your trapped paw
should have stepped across. You said "there is no lead -

open the door", and after several seconds
I felt you wanted me to guide you through
the gate, whispering *salida's* double truth,
that as you leave one cage another beckons.

# Boleo

*In Argentine tango, a Boleo is a swivel about an axis on one foot;*
*in an embellished form, the second foot can trail,*
*drawing a sweeping arc across the dance floor*

I once laid out a set of flower beds
by driving pegs to the shape of The Great Bear
and, using twine of varied lengths, carved
great intersecting curves to guide the cuts.

On this morning after a night of dance,
rearranging chairs and potted plants,
I see the circles darkened by the dew,
knowing that the perfect arc was you.

So in my garden heaven I will place
you at the seven star-points, watching the graceful
way you sweep your heel in a slow *boleo*,
marking out our bed with a cold stiletto.

# Mordida

*Mordida - the "little bite", where a tango dancer sandwiches
a partner's foot between his/her own. Pasada - stepping
over another's outstretched or trapping foot.*

Fourteen beats is a long time ahead
to plan my hidden ploy behind a smile,
counting down the steps. But, when I'm ready,

I'll set the trap - the simple glide and slide
to stop you, sensing your defiant stare
as I snare you with my shoes, your foot inside

my leather cage. So would it really scare
you if you knew that this was not a game
to me - that in my fantasies you wear

a frock of fur, your clamped leg maimed and lame
so you can never run? It's a facade -
we both know that you cannot be tamed,

or shackled by my minted breath for, as hard
as I try, it's not enough to make you stay,
escaping with an arrogant *pasada*,
no longer forced to feel the fear of prey.

# Ochos

Ochos - *A set of tango steps in which the follower marks
a figure-of-eight on the floor, with ankles touching on each turn.*

I asked you whether you could see my face
or whether you had tango danced as I
stored your stick. The way you found my eyes
by homing in made me feel like fresh prey.

We stood within the centre of the room
so you could feel the counter-clockwise breeze
from the scented skirts and freshly minted breath,
and the stink of men, of spent testosterone.

We tried to walk but you said you had never
made a backward step in all your life.
Because you only moved towards the light,
you wavered like a moth. I asked you whether

you'd ever felt the poise of the ballerina
on a jewelry box, the way her touching feet
turned to the lullaby, no sense of fear.
That this was what you were - a figurine.

As the music played you swayed to the rhythm,
legs like wooden staves pegged to the floor,
your *terra firma* that kept you from the jaws
of the terror of the fall, your grounded prison.

I whispered "figurine", then moved your weight
onto the right, the pivot then the slide
back of the left leg, the gliding step and the slight
turn, the first loop of the figure-of-eight.

-/-

The room is blind to her smile as she leaves to start
her journey home, invisible to all
those eyes in streets and cars; but now the walls
echo to her taps, her new staccato.

# Eight

Watching the way you dance *ochos*
to Piazzolla's slow tangos
my eyes trace the figure-of-eight
of your steps and skirt. And I'm dazed,
like the first time I heard Django
Reinhardt's *Nuage* and the magical
eighth note, perfect to the power
of *yotta* - but a minor-7th.

*Yotta (Y) is the largest prefix in SI units,*
*as in $1000^8$ (one Quadrillion)*

# Barrida

*In Argentine tango, where one person's foot sweeps the other's foot across the floor and places it without losing contact; when perfect, it is not possible to discern who is leading or who is following.*

The feet lock like two poles of a magnet,
moments held in time, joined at the shoe-hip,
tempting each to move before the magic
slide, as though they were tied by strands of music.

Perhaps he's helping her across a field
of mines, her mind lost in loss and thought,
or forcing his will until her body yields,
or simply saving the precious bones of her foot.

That's what he'd like to think, but she is the one
who's dragging the ego'd foot of a fool towards her,
pulling his leathered lap-dog lust by its tongue
as she leads his love-blinded shoe to water.

# Gancho

*A movement in tango when a dancer hooks a leg*
*sharply around or between a partner's legs.*

The look on your face as your leg
hooks back behind my knee
is one of barbed disdain,
your back straight and your head
turned away from me,
your eyes closed in pain.

But there is a moment
                    within a slow movement
when time seems to close,
                    as though the music chose
to sleep inside a dream.

And then in slow motion
                    with feline devotion
your calf strokes my thigh
                    and to my surprise
your mouth is edged with cream.

# Volcadas

*In Argentine tango, a Volcada ("falling step") is a move in which
the leader causes the follower to lean forward and fall off her axis
before catching her again. From the verb Volcar - to tip-over, or capsize.*

Her feet are points of nautical dividers,
sounding out the measure of their route
in swooning gyroscopic steps, her axis
blind to he who rights her lilting lightness,
knowing he has fixed a course.
                                    Could you
trust me this much? Of course, I'm really asking
would you ever truly trust me: would you
stand in a wailing storm on a wave-washed deck
without a rail because I said the sea
was mine; or faint in the wind because you knew
I would be waiting to take your weight with my neck?
I don't expect you to forget the wretched
dance that fated night, but will you please
give me one last chance and fall for me?

# Vareador

*A tango dancer who is clumsy or inconsiderate
who "might as well be walking a horse"*

Watching as you turn in his embrace
reminds me of my mother's Zimmer frame
driving her knuckles wild, her crumpled face
watching. As you turn in his embrace
searching for your seat, there's not a trace
of grace left - backing up, taking aim,
watching as you turn in. His embrace
reminds me of my mother's Zimmer frame.

# Reflections

# The Color of Tango

So here was color, vibrant shades that shimmered and set a tone of light and sound out of sight of the still world outside. The door that night was an iridescent iris, the winter left behind to its silence and this sense that here was the past of everything almost touched, simmered down to its essence, ready now, ready.

*Red*: Flushed faces, never smacked or slapped, some with heat and others blushing over errors, stare beyond their breath, arms wrapped as tight as teenage love, their shared pheromones squeezed up and out, resting in their necks, erect and taut against the rush, the terror of the turns, the sharp looks teetering on one side of a line of violence. *Violet*: In her hair a single flower rests in waves, teasing in that come-and-get-me way she always used, the way she used me - paper petals on a white gown later torn in the final days, and the way that single chard of confetti stuck like static to the back of the only photograph that hadn't died - I could frame her beauty. *Blue*: Men stalk the floor: the aged lady in the dress suit, eyes lacquered to black palms, or she with eyes open on her partner's cheek, or the young ones full of fury, and the divorcee who sweats low on her spine where the hand rests. The waiting ladies sit and talk across each other's patience, seeing all except within the blue depths - staying his entrance, sliding his shoes into view, the rest unseen. *Green*: Look through his eyes, look down the dark arms to the fingers tapping his groin like waking the dead, and the slow shake of the table, the way he lingers on the swollen glass, leaning back into shyness, this green tanguero who's never danced before. And this is me, this is my shadow. *Yellow*: Or is this the next page? I guess you reach an age when the world will never say you smell of urine, when the leaves of lettuce from your Subway soft baguette relieve the sight of the ground stubs of your teeth which match the jaundiced lychee of your eyes, a melanoma time when, as you bravely stumble to the next dance, no one answers no - you answered no. *Indigo*: Fresh from some safari trip filled with dripped coins of guilt, her tie-dyed tied sarong hitched to her earth-mother hips, she sips a single 10oz shot of organic merlot, one hand to her lips searching for her last cigarette, smelling of bush, smelling the fresh bushmeat of the night, eying prey with the third eye, no panty hose just bites, quite strange. *Orange*: Never rhymes, never mind, the glow above the washroom door is always warm and sly - like a long time ago in the Ruperra Pub in Cardiff's Tiger Bay, a light would flash in the bar each time a condom was removed. I heard her say "you'll be fucking lucky" as he slid back beside her; the only one who didn't laugh just sat there in his beer, stopped at amber.

I could have told you of the other colors: the steel-grey stilettos that flashed and slashed, the faded jade bracelet that swung with each frenzied turn, the turquoise tufts that stood up from the heels brushing taut calves, the lust of lust, the gamboge parquet floor, the skirts and skirts whirling and whirling in thrilling shocking-hot-flamingo-pink, the sleepy lids of razzle-dazzle rose and twilight lavender, and the taupe'd men all dull and dark who talked in sullen monotones. Instead, you entered, you with the necklace of seven stones, bearing all the weight and lifting all their hues and lives into the prism of your throat so that, when you took his hand and graced the floor, there was only whiteness and all around you paled to pastel shades. In the night you left outside, the streets sulked and waited in their drained monochrome.

# Milonga - Haikus

*Moments in a formal tango dance ...*

my neck
where her head will rest
coolness of cologne

laced shoes
await the first tanda
tongues tied

he scans the room
while she's lost in reverie —
spouses' dance

this is the dance
she waits for in the shadows
he who never asks

she declines his glance
with a slow turn of the head
moment of death

I am that dancer
who watches you
empty arms

I capture the eye
that will soon brush my cheek
black lashes

wetness
low on her spine
from other dancers' hands

on your axis
almost imperceptible
a waver

gazes locked
the beating of my heart ...
you leave me breathless

hook and kick —
your stiletto guards
my tango cage

you end the spin
your skirt wraps my thighs
like a hot sarong

a jolt of pain
in her left foot ...
from her curt thank you

the bandoneón dies
doors open into the night
taillights fade ...

# Waiting with Water

*In Argentine tango, men can queue to dance with the most elegant ladies,
stopping them before they are able to return to their seats.*

Watching you
impeccably polite
taking each offered hand
one arm trailing back
to where I sit
holding your water
your movements drained
by each new man
your face tightening
around a wan smile
until the time you glance away
and dance your way
to the cool of a chair
hair matted into your neck
freckled beads on your lips
your legs splayed
body slumped forward
clutching the crumpled cup
I fan you with my breath

# Walking to You - a Triolet

One night I'll walk across the room for you.
I'll open up. My love, one evening soon,
will simmer, boiling down my life to
one night. I'll walk across the room for you,
rolling up my sleeves to show a new
me ... perhaps. That's what I told the moon
one night - *I'll walk across the room*. For you,
I'll open up my love one evening soon.

# Chico Frumboli

*Chico Frumboli does not look like a typical dancer,*
*but he is one of the leading tango exponents of the world.*

I packing on the weight,
growing a pony tail
tied with a band of sweat,
boasting a beard, a stud
in the open left ear.
My jackets have no buttons -
double-breasted, gaping
with matching shirts and chest,
and paneled, flanneled pants
crumpled down on spats
improbably white and worn.

Her patience has been worn
down by spiteful spats,
rants and spittled pants
and groans, my toupee'd chest
hair like a gaping
velcro vest. But on
the other hand I have no ear
for music - just an aged stud
looking to spread his seed and sweat.
So to dance like you, with a tail
wind? - she'll have to wait
                until I lose some weight.

# Washing up at 2.15 am

*A tanguera is a lady tango dancer, a lady*

Even on the phone
I knew the state you were in,
the sound of running water
and the slick slap as you moved
the piece from hand to sticky hand -
dirty stinking men with grown-up daughters,
the sink still thirsts for them.

Funny, you ought to
have known, but then -
I should have known
that in your land the men douche
with a hose on cock and hole,
rinsing down the drops until the evening
heat dries all.

"Do men use tissues then?" - I've never seen a crumpled dove
                in a washroom bin.
"But do they wash?" - a few, depending how successful they have been,
                the piece can slip inside untouched.
"And if they don't or won't? - they cup a hand for privacy and shake,
                just long enough to stop the stares and grunts.

So sorry this is how you learned.
For me, I wash and scrub
and, as I dry, I slide
a wetted finger over lips
as though they were your lips.
This is the risk
*tangueras* face -
hands too low in the back,
the lump that matches the one in your throat,
the stench from nylon shirts
            too tight for flirting with the night.

Count the beats they're gone
and if the door is still ajar when they return
or the same song is playing
its soulful end, you'll know.
You'd look so fine in gloves my love,
much better than being stroked by fellows
with yellow fingers who never smoke.

# Tango Tankas

standing in a grove
of aspens as the Autumn
winds dance with the trees
the golden leaves shimmering
to the sound of tango skirts


dancing alone
my arms wrapped around the night
the music echos
through this space
where you should be


walking up to her
still clasping her tango shoes
she nods to my eyes
rising up on 4" heels
dress stretched in parts forbidden


closing the embrace
your arm draped around my neck
it's always the same
hair filled with terror
like a cat dancing with ghosts


fingers in her back
pressing the spinal buttons
under her bonnet
she purrs her final warning
before the tango fur flies

sliding over silk
his hands coax waves of static
electricity
driving her slow boleos
into his magnetic arms


when you danced away
the faint scent on my shoulder
evaporated
into the sulking darkness
looking for another's arms


the music now dead
shoes are placed in shopping bags
feet flat to the floor
the ladies stepped down from grace
men's socks leaving spoor of sweat


on Freedom Plaza
traffic cops and tourists stretch
their fat rubbernecks
straining to see the tango
arms folded across their souls


since her husband died
nights are faces in the fire
their eyes turned away
touching others in her sight
like all those late milongas

# 4.6692016090

I am strangely attracted to the thought that the
    Feigenbaum Constant
could bring non-linear order to my life. The way
the same tune plays at dawn the instant

my chaotic clock starts - I call it my butterfly
effect - groundhogs would sigh with causal relief
at the degrees of freedom of their own days
    within days

Have you ever noticed how young trees are relieved
of the choice of growth by randomly budding branches
and veins, basking in the false belief

of free will, blind to Poincaré's mapped chances
in the endless search for light and life? But life
hangs on a power law and tango dances

to the beat of earth's bandoneón which writhes
and riles against the magma music within it.
Mandelbrot was right - that a fractal defines
a line, this endless song, that is truly infinite.

# Milonga - El Mesón

**Santa Fe, New Mexico**

*A milonga ia a formal tango dance*

You can tell a lot
from the way they're parked
    or dumped,
reflections of their owners
    stepping out ...

Reserved up-front, 2-wheel drive Mercedes of
revamped widow wanabees ready to spin on ice;
spattered flat-beds, one wheel on the sidewalk, macho-
mechanistic, grinding forward, oblivious;
150,000 miles away, clunker cars stained and drained
by past lovers and children, wanting to start again;
zippy Minis, squeezed in tight, stick shift stuck
in a lower gear, whining like stunted runts;
paid up SUVs, air-conditioned to a death
of comfort, looking to be looked up to;
and Harleys, cock-sured to the side, chromed heads
turned away, tassled arms waiting.
And all stream tired ...

a line of seeming who-be-nots,
shuffling, shyly looking for shoes
in Wallmart bags and Hilda Palladino totes
and ruck-sacks bloodied by the Sangre de Cristos:

builders with blubbered hands scrubbed raw,
trinket shop assistants bathed in baubles,
doctors, nurses, patient
therapists and zen wonder-workers

and wounded housewives with tongues like knives.
And then the opening ...

The women in their 4" heels, calves yoga'd to ovals
like muscled mangos melting into ankles
held by sinews grafted to necks, erect, watching,
waiting to be watched, skirts ready to catch fire.

The men stalking forward like cuban-heeled cats,
an outstretched hand, a stare, the nod, curdled
smiles in the glare of the floor, the grace of the embrace
laced with the first purple notes of *Pugliese*.

In the low-lit glow of the back-room bar
friends and strangers who may never have touched
slide and glide through blind songs,
legs wrapping and flicking, spinning in each other's space,
the women stepping over fences of feet,
turning inside arms that slide across adobe bones.

My shoes are resting,
a pair of *Tango Brujo* bigoteras itching to move.
But sitting in my snow-boots, looking through
a glass of Rioja, you are not there.
And the room takes on a crimson hue,
figures moving in and out, distorted but lovely,
elongated by the lens, to vanish past the lip,
to end the night bubble-wrapped and furred,
        searching ...

for each other's cars, never noticing
the fresh treads in snow,

the arced scars and ruts in the road,
the fog of tell-tale sweat on glass,

secrets huddled in hoods,
the creaks and cracks of engines cooling.

# Libertango Duet

after Astor Piazzolla

*A milonga is a formal tango dance in which men*
*ask ladies to dance with their eyes.*

I search the room for you, at each milonga.
The secret scent of you is getting stronger
amid the stream of heat, the steam of dancers
whose minds are there to cheat. Their furtive glances
look to another's eyes, another tanda,
to seek a bigger prize, the hand of candor
that, in a close embrace, *ocho cortado*
as lovers face-to-face; and two *sacadas*.

And in the silent depths they wait forever.
They sit in rows bereft, their feet together.
He walks up like a God – why did he choose *her*?
His eyes meet hers, she nods. His eyes peruse her,
his five-dance trophy wife, nine minute partner.
They join the dance of life, his role to guard her.
I search the room for you at this milonga
for just a scent of you to feed my hunger.

Then in the room
I search the room for you, at each milonga.
a hint of your perfume,
The secret scent of you is getting stronger
There
amid the stream of heat, the steam of dancers
the silent shimmer of your hair.
whose minds are there to cheat. Their furtive glances
Your eyes,

52

look to another's eyes, another tanda,
those eyes that dance and flirt.
to seek a bigger prize, the hand of candor
And the glide,
that, in close embrace, *ocho cortado*
the cool breath from your skirts.
as lovers face-to-face; and two *sacadas*.


And I
And in the silent depths they wait forever.
watch your every move.
They sit in rows bereft, their feet together.
I die,
He walks up like a God – why did he choose *her*?
die each time you take the floor.
His eyes meet hers, she nods. His eyes peruse her,
In his arms
his five-dance trophy wife, nine minute partner.
I love you even more,
They join the dance of life, his role to guard her.
ever more,
I search the room for you at this milonga
as storm before the calm
for just a scent of you to feed my hunger.


And then you
    are alone
    for me.
I catch your eye, see you smile.
You stare and ask me where I've been –
Beyond my life and in your dreams.

I searched the rooms for you at each milonga
and as I longed for you, my love grew stronger.
But now in close embrace to Piazzolla,
my arm around your waist, yours on my shoulder,
I feel your every breath when we *parada*,
the skin within your dress when you *cruzada*.
Your lashes kiss my cheek, and so alive we
Step out with tango feet … into our life.

# Milonga - Wesley Methodist Church

*A milonga is a formal tango dance*

Curled up in the corner of the room
like stop-start fools, another night of doomed

trips and skips, each tango seemed
a never-ending toil, the hallowed dream

to end the dance as one, of breathing the same
breath, beyond our boiled cheeks of shame.

But then, with no warning, the off-beat months faded
away into the worn pews of the faithful

as, in a slow turn, your body entered
mine, while mine melted into your center

with flashes of static, and this fantastic sense
that we had stepped through a cloud of incense

into a new world. And it was like this. It was like

the divine release of the first stroke of a water
color, like waking from a life of sleep-walking
to one where the dream is real, the sublime wonder
of choking on your own heart, the monad miracle
of moving as one spirit, our arms melded
into the shape of a ship.
                              I am no longer a follower
of God, a lame lickspit to a leader
who killed my own. On that night, no
sea of guilt could sink the sacred moment.

In that moment there was no leader or follower,
just a melded miracle of wonder, like walking on water.

# A Lesson for Sons

I've taught you all I know about the world,
the way that life can bite you in the arse,
and good ol' Sod's Law says that pretty girls
will go for ugly guys with wads and cars.
But now it's time to leave the clubs and bars
and learn to tango dance. Let me allay
your fears: the dance is all, and no one cares
except for cultured etiquette and nails.
So be aware: you'll have to shave each day
and wear cologne from London or Paris.
And garlic bread is out, and so is ale ...
but vodka has no smell. For this, there'll be
no stains in under-arms of shirts and, best,
you'll never have such cleansing nightmare sweats.

# La Cumparisita

*In tango milongas (formal dances), La Cumparisita is traditionally
the last song of the evening; dancers reserve this for their significant others.
Men ask ladies to dance with their eyes.*

He wants to stop, to shout her name aloud
for evening's end has caught him by surprise.
And then he sees her moving through the crowd,

a flash of colored silk, not like the shroud
he's dancing with ... who knows his nod implies
he wants to stop. To shout her name aloud

would break a rule, for speech is not allowed
except for jilted sobs and whispered sighs.
And then he sees her moving through the crowd

within another's arms, her cowed head bowed,
as a cloud descends of jealousy and lies.
He wants to stop, to shout her name aloud,

to break their close embrace, to fill his proud
bravado face with bile. The music dies,
and then he sees her. Moving through the crowd

he loses her from sight, but knows she vowed
to keep *Cumparisita* for his eyes.
He wants to stop, to shout her name aloud.
And then he sees her moving through the crowd.

the bandoneón dies
doors open into the night
taillights fade …

# Acknowledgements

This book describes a journey of a life-long 'sitter-outer' of any form of dancing, from the initial idea and decision to start to learn to dance tango, through the first year's struggles and occasional ecstasy with the dance. I would like to think the journey has only just begun.

Nothing in this book would have been possible without the kind and often stern perseverance of my teacher Dima Berk of Tango Red - in every tango lesson I learned lessons beyond the dance, lessons within lessons, and some of these thoughts appear in these poems. But most of all I would like to thank my dance partner, Layla Kassem, for without her I would have neither danced beyond the second lesson, nor had the honesty to write what she has always told me to write.

Poems in this collection have appeared in 14 by14, Decanto, Modern Haiku, New Mexico Poetry Review, The Raintown Review, Ribbons, Science Poetry and Shaking Like a Mountain.

Lew Watts is originally from Wales and, after many years living in Africa, the Middle East and Europe, moved recently to the United Sates where he is an energy consultant. His poetry has been published in various magazines and anthologies in Europe, and his first US work appeared in 2010. For almost 2 years, he has been learning to dance Tango and his experiences inspired this, his first, poetry collection. He lives in Santa Fe and Chicago and travels extensively.